2/02

SO-AJM-360

It's Best to Leave a Snake Alone

By Allan Fowler

Consultants:

Robert L. Hillerich, Ph.D., Bowling Green
State University, Bowling Green, Ohio

Mary Nalbandian, Director of Science,
Chicago Public Schools, Chicago, Illinois

Fay Robinson, Child Development Specialist

CHILDRENS PRESS ®

CHICAGO

Design by Beth Herman Design Associates

Library of Congress Cataloging-in-Publication Data

Fowler, Allan
It's best to leave a snake alone / by Allan Fowler.
    p. cm. −(Rookie read-about science)
    Summary: A simple description of the physical characteristics
and behavior of snakes
    ISBN 0-516-04926-7
    1.Snakes–Juvenile literature.
    [1. Snakes] I. Title. II. Series: Fowler, Allan. Rookie read-about science.
QLL666.06F58 1992
597.96–dc20   91-39245
                                           CIP
                                           AC

Snakes look slimy.

But have you ever touched
one at a zoo?

If you have, then you
know that snakes feel dry.

Many snakes are beautiful.
Some have bright stripes or
other interesting designs.

Snakes don't have any legs. They slide around on their bellies.

Most kinds of snakes, like this garter snake, don't hurt people.

Some snakes are even
helpful. They eat rats,
mice, and other animals
that destroy farmers' crops.

Snakes also eat insects
and worms, fish, birds,
and smaller snakes.

Snakes belong to a group of animals called reptiles. Lizards, turtles, alligators, and crocodiles are also reptiles.

Snakes live in woods or fields, in water or in deserts. They don't live where it's too cold.

A snake's skin is made
of many connected pieces
called scales.

A couple of times each year, a snake's outer skin comes off–and there's a new skin underneath!

Where are a snake's ears?
It hasn't any.

But a snake can still tell
if something is moving
anywhere near it.
It feels the movement
through the ground.

A snake uses its forked tongue to smell things.

Some snakes are poisonous. They can make you very sick if they bite you.

A poisonous snake has
long teeth called fangs.
It squirts the poison
through its fangs.

Cobras, coral snakes, copperheads, and water moccasins are poisonous.

So are rattlesnakes.

A rattlesnake shakes the rattle in its tail to scare off enemies.

The rattling sound is a warning that the snake might bite.

Some big snakes, such
as pythons and boas,
wrap themselves around
an animal and squeeze it
to death.

How big are pythons?
They can be more than
30 feet long!

But don't worry—snakes
that big live only in jungles
far away from here.

If you want to see dangerous snakes–like rattlesnakes and cobras and pythons–the best place is at the zoo.

Sonoran Sidewinder
Crotalus cerastes cercobombus
Range: southwestern
United States

27

Snakes you might see
in the woods and fields
around your home
probably won't hurt you.

But it's always best to
leave a snake alone ...
just in case!

Words You Know

python

garter snake

poisonous snakes

cobra

coral snake

copperhead

water moccasin

rattlesnake

30

reptiles

lizards

turtles

alligators

crocodiles

scales

fangs

Index

About the Author

Allan Fowler is a free-lance writer with a background in advertising. Born in New York, he lives in Chicago now and enjoys traveling.

Photo Credits

©Busch Gardens, Tampa, 1991– 24-25

©James P. Rowan– 27

Tom Stack & Associates– ©Joe McDonald, 19, 30 (center left); ©David M. Dennis, 30 (center center); ©John Cancalosi, 30 (bottom left)

Valan– ©Jim Merli, Cover, 5, 16, 18, 31 (bottom); ©M. Julien, 4; ©Jeff Foott, 6; ©Joseph R. Pearce, 7, 30 (top right); ©John Mitchell, 8, 22, 30 (center right); ©John Cancalosi, 9, 12, 15, 21, 30 (top left and bottom right); ©Stephen J. Krasemann, 10, 31 (center left); ©Dennis W. Schmidt, 11; ©Aubrey Lang, 13; ©Tom W. Parkin, 28; ©F. Yuwono, 31 (top left); ©Wayne Lankinen, 31 (top right); ©Joyce Photographics, 31 (center right)

COVER: Emerald Tree Boa